When Hard Times Come

Dudley Hall

KERYGMA VENTURES PRESS

Euless, Texas

When Hard Times Come

Copyright © 2012 by Kerygma Ventures

Published by   Kerygma Ventures Press
              P.O. Box 101
              Euless, Texas 76039

Cover Design: Inprov, Inc.

ISBN 978-1-937833-03-9

Printed in the United States of America

To my wife, Betsy Hall

I have been truly blessed to be married to Betsy for 43 years. She has inspired me by her unusual capability to lead when needed and to follow without complaint. She has faced the sun as well as the storms with utmost confidence in God. Her life inspires me.

Acknowledgments

I would especially like to thank all of the subscribers to Dudley's Monthly Message. Through the years you have been an inspiration, a point of accountability and a wonderful audience to whom I preach the messages God has placed in my heart. I consider you family. You've heard these messages in some form or fashion before; I hope you are blessed and God speaks to you and encourages you as you read them here.

Thanks to Tom Hall for compilation and editing support. Karis McCollum and David Hall also edited the manuscript. The errors that remain are not for a lack of trying. In addition, Karis provided a great deal of administrative support and David took the book through the publishing process. I appreciate all the help and support.

Table of Contents

Introduction..1

1. Facing the Giants 3

   The Nature of the Battle 4

   The Greater David 6

   The Benefits for Believers... 8

2. Deliberate Calm 11

   Find Calm before Choosing Action 13

   The Privilege of Seeing the Unseen 15

   Deliberate Calm Provides a New Perspective.......... 18

3. More Grace at Ziklag...21

   David and Ziklag Again 22

   The Privilege of Access... 23

   Recalling God's Faithfulness 24

   Blessed Beyond Any Doubt 27

4. Kingdom Economics..29

   The King Alone Determines the Outcomes 30

   Kingdom of Covenant 31

   Fatherly Kingdom 32

   The Influence of the Faithful.................................... 35

Servants Are the Greatest 36

5. Why Does Victory Feel Like Defeat?............................39

False Prophets Expose Immaturity 41

Who Creates False Prophets? 44

God's Design: Exalt Jesus through Weaknesses 45

Conclusion 49

Introduction

We all tend to dream and fantasize about life without trouble; we would like to think that there is a state of mind or even a place in life where hard times never come. Some people have decided to find that place or state and seem so determined that they will even suspend reality to find it. Christians have sometimes been led to believe that if they try hard enough or believe strongly enough, they will be rescued from trouble, obstacles, and hard times. They tend to judge themselves and others rather harshly for not knowing the secret or achieving the goal. They feel sure the next novel insight or the next radical commitment will get them over the hump.

God doesn't offer escape as his solution to difficulty, but rather grace. The grace provided through the gospel of Jesus Christ embraces trouble and transforms it into a display case for God's glory. Those who have come to know him personally will inevitably change their goal in life from one of personal ease to one of glorifying God. Once they have tasted the sweetness of living for another, the taste of ease and comfort as the essence of life becomes bitter. They long to live in grace—and grace excels in the midst of difficulty.

When Adam and Eve fell in the Garden of Eden, their perspective (as well as ours) was distorted. Blocked from seeing clearly through eyes of faith, all of humanity sees through eyes of distrust. Since we are not fully convinced that God is completely good or totally in control, we misinterpret the circumstances of life and adopt a concept of reality far different from God's perspective. God uses trouble to expose our faulty perspective and reveal his corrected perspective. He then empowers us to live from that new perspective by granting to us his very life. Everyday becomes a window of discovery as we unpack the treasure of eternal life. In the following pages we will examine how God gets us to his reality and what is included in the great treasures.

1. Facing the Giants

The prophet Samuel anointed David as king when David was still a young man. Saul remained in office and eventually became quite jealous of David. For about 13 years, David endured one climactic experience after another that prepared him for his ultimate destiny. It was critical that David knew how to act like God's king before he received the crown. Saul was proof enough that crowning an unprepared candidate didn't work. This time God installed the king, and he did it through the process of gradual preparation. David's anointing alone was not enough for him to rule effectively. He had to discover real authority through the crucible of weakness and faith. God would expose his weaknesses and reveal the corresponding grace.

The biblical story in 1 Samuel 17 is familiar. A war had been going on for some time between God's people (Israel) and their pagan neighbors (the Philistines). Jesse's older boys were part of the struggle; meanwhile David was back at home, still watching the sheep for his dad. One day Jesse asked David to take some food and refreshments to his

brothers on the battlefield. When David arrived he discovered the true nature of the battle. The "champion" of the
Philistines was challenging the "champion" of Israel.
Goliath was about nine feet tall. He carried a giant sword
and spear and his armor weighed more than 100 pounds.
Every day he came out to mock the Israelites, demanding
they send their best man to fight him.

The Nature of the Battle

This scene bothered David. He saw that in reality it was
a battle between the name of God and the names of the gods
of fear. He was offended for the reputation of God, who had
adopted Israel as his own people. It looked like the God of
the Israelites was weak. David was showing early signs of a
royal perspective. It didn't take long for David to catch the
rumor circulating among the soldiers that King Saul would
reward anyone who would fight the Philistine champion
with marriage to his daughter, riches, and tax-free living.
David offered to fight the giant, even as his brothers mocked
him. It was a difference in his perspective that produced
courage that the others didn't have. David didn't see an
intimidating giant; he saw an enemy of truth. Though
hesitant to trust a boy, Saul had no other takers. He offered
to give David his royal armor, but David quickly realized he
could not wear the armor of the previous administration. He
was a new king destined to rule a new kingdom a new way.

As he reassured Saul, David remembered the faithfulness of God on his behalf when the bears and lions came

against the sheep he protected. At that time he had represented his father, Jesse, and God had given him success in his responsibilities. Now, he would represent God against another foe, and he was confident God would work on his behalf again. His anointing was now connecting with his assignment. There was about to be a happening! David was engaging in a battle God had some interest in. Instead of trusting the armor of Saul, he used the skills that he had incidentally developed in his previous job. He took his sling, picked up five smooth stones and ran toward Goliath, who was trash-talking the little boy with the sling. (Some wits have suggested David actually visualized the girl Saul had promised, and that's what got him running.) As David released the stone, it was guided to the only vulnerable spot on Goliath's body. The stone sank deep into his skull and the champion dropped like . . . well, like a dead man. David approached the fallen giant and used the very sword of his enemy to cut off the head of Goliath and carry it back with him as a trophy.

The Israelite soldiers surrounding the field saw what had happened and took courage. They took advantage of their champion's victory and began routing the Philistines. They chased them for miles and gathered up the spoils. David acted like a true king that day, while the reigning king was too fearful to fight. David was being prepared for the day when he would have not only the anointing and the assignment of a king, but also the appropriate acknowledgement.

The Greater David

This is one of many times David serves as a type of a greater David who would one day reign on the throne of God over the whole creation. While this story contains nuggets of truth we could mine to encourage us to act in boldness to face our giants, in essence that approach misses the point. The good news of this story relates to Jesus and what he has won for us. David's model is inspiring, but apart from the obvious presence of God, "Goliaths" make us run for cover. We need more than moral principles gleaned from this text. We need to see Jesus.

Like David, who was hidden in the fields tending sheep ignored by his father and brothers, Jesus grew up in obscurity. He lived in a small town called Nazareth where he was accused of being a bastard and had no remarkable qualifications. Among many itinerate teachers roaming the hills of Judea, he was just one more. As David was faithful to work for his father Jesse, representing him well by taking seriously his responsibilities, Jesus also spent almost 30 years working with Joseph in the carpenter shop. For both it seemed too long to wait while the circumstances continued to worsen. David was anointed when he was about thirteen and had to wait for the job to open. Jesus was born a king but waited for the day of his appointment.

David went out to fight the enemy's champion as representative of God's people. All Israel stepped onto the field in the form of one man—and a young one at that. Jesus also represented the people of God. He was called Son of Man, identifying with mankind as the last Adam. He was also called Son of God, referring to his identity with Israel. He lived and died to fulfill the destiny of both mankind and Israel. David instinctively knew his assignment: he could not allow the name of God to be mocked. Confident of his anointing, David stepped toward his assignment and won the victory. Jesus knew early on that he would be about his Father's business. He knew he was sent from God and would go back to God. This knowledge of who he was and what he was to do allowed him to wash the disciples feet and to die a sacrificial death.

David had to survive against a rejected king. Saul, having been rejected by God, was determined to persecute and destroy the new regime. Jesus likewise came to his own and they rejected him, because God had already rejected them. They had made an idol of the law and the customs of the Jewish leaders, who hounded Jesus until his death and then hounded his disciples until 70 AD when their city and temple were finally destroyed.

Saul's armor wouldn't fit David just as the customs of Israel's traditions would not fit Jesus. Jesus refused to be defined or confined by the legalistic interpretations of God's laws. Jesus knew he was the temple and would not idolize buildings and teachings that shrouded the true image of the Father. David was very interested in the girl who would become his wife as a result of defeating the champion. Jesus is very interested in his bride. He died to forgive her sins and lives to perfect her in every way. Both David and Jesus get the girl. (Actually David didn't get the first daughter, but a younger one. Jesus didn't get the first daughter, Israel; he got the Church, made up of Jews and Gentiles.)

David used what he had, a stone and a sling. Jesus used what he had, who he was. He was both man and God, both humble and submissive. Daniel the prophet had seen a vision about a stone being cut out of a mountain without human hands. It rolled down the mountain and destroyed the kingdoms of the earth while setting up an everlasting kingdom of God's people. Jesus was himself that stone. He declared that those who fell on it would be broken (all to their good), but the stone would crush those who rejected it.

The Benefits for Believers

David used Goliath's own sword to cut off his head. When Satan walked the valleys of man's heart swinging the hundred-pound sword called death, he ruled the day with his threat. But Jesus took death upon himself and by it defeated Satan.

Since therefore the children share in flesh and blood, he himself likewise partook of the same things, that through death he might destroy the one who has the power of death, that is, the devil, and deliver all those who through fear of death were subject to lifelong slavery.

Hebrews 2:14-15

David could confidently say, "Yea, though I walk through the valley of the shadow of death I will fear no evil . . . " And Jesus could boldly say, "No one takes my life. I lay it down." So Christians can exultingly say, "O death where is your sting? O grave where is your victory?" The greater David has faced death's champion and cut off his head. He has also come to live within the people of God who can now appropriate his life. There is something in us all that must be akin to the courage that arose in the hearts of David's brothers when they saw the giant fall. We want to rout the enemy and take the spoils. It is our heritage. We can now face the giants of our own existence by trusting in the victorious Champion who lives within us.

Let's embrace the promise found in this text. David's example is a good model, but we don't live in David's time. We are not fighting a nine-foot tall Goliath; the Philistines aren't really our problem; and we have not been anointed by Samuel to be king over God's people.

David is a shadow of Jesus the substance who represents all those who are "in Him." The big Goliath that strikes fear in the hearts of all people is Satan. He claims that because we have broken the eternal law of God, we deserve to die. He is anxious to carry out that sentence. This fear of death arising from our consciousness of guilt drives our lives. Until this sentence is removed, we are paralyzed. Like the army of Israel, we feel alienated from holy God, disqualified to do battle with spiritual forces, and fearful that we will lose at whatever we do.

However, our champion has defeated that enemy. Satan's weapons have been stripped from him. Jesus has fulfilled the covenant God made with Israel. He has paid the full penalty for our violating God's laws. He has defeated death by his own resurrection and now sits in full authority over his people guaranteeing everything touching them will have their good as its end (Romans 8:28-31).

We are no longer paralyzed by fear. We can enforce our champion's victory by living as his people to reflect his glory, confident that he is eager to give us what we need to accomplish our assignment. We don't have to try to act like David; we can gratefully receive what David/Jesus won for us. His presence with us is the confidence that nothing can separate us from the Fatherly love, and that alone frees us to be who we are.

Satan continues to lie and to accuse, but Jesus is truth. Jesus blesses instead of accusing. Death still happens to the physical bodies, but now it has been transformed into a door opening to life characterized by resurrection. Battles still rage, but our champion sits on a throne making sure every detail of our lives is soaked with more grace than we need.

2. Deliberate Calm

As hard as we may try, we cannot plan or prepare well enough to avoid the turbulence that comes from living in a fallen and broken world. And when everything around us is shaking, we need to find a place of calm – not merely a plan for escape. We are looking for more than relief. We are responsible to affect our circumstances, not just survive them.

The story of David's experience at Ziklag in 1 Samuel 30, provides an intriguing case study. Although he had been anointed king by Samuel, the prophet, David spent almost fourteen years trying to avoid Saul, the rejected king who was still on the throne and jealously pursued David. During that time, David worked alongside the Philistines, helping them fight their enemies. As a reward he had been given the city of Ziklag by the king of the Philistines. One day he came home to discover that the Amalekites had burned his city and taken everything, including his wives. David was understandably distressed, and the men were threatening to stone him. So, the Scripture tells us, "David strengthened himself in the Lord his God" (v. 6). He then went to the priest to determine what course of action he should take. What did David know that caused him to stop in this moment of crisis and first strengthen himself in the Lord?

Neuroscientists tell us that in threatening situations we all experience fear. Some panic while others move into a deliberate calm researchers call metacognition. These people can think about where they are and what they should really be concerned about. Pilots are trained to handle emergences with deliberate calm. Military leaders learn to face crises with the same superior awareness. I recently spoke with a retired military officer who had listened to many tapes of soldiers' last words. For instance, one helicopter pilot said, "We are taking fire and the ship is going down. I expect no survivors. Good day." Another squad leader who was trapped in open space by Taliban forces said, "We are taking direct fire. We're in the open without cover. We cannot survive. It has been an honor serving under you, sir."

Metacognition in combat is a result of conscious choices and constant practice. That is what leadership training is all about. Pilots spend hours in simulators learning to think about thinking during emergencies. We were all impressed on January 15, 2009, when Captain "Sully" Sullenberger safely ditched his Airbus A320 in the Hudson River after both engines flamed out from striking a flock of geese shortly after take off. He had mere seconds to make life-saving decisions for his crew and passengers—155 people in all. He couldn't afford panic or paralysis in the face of threatening circumstances.

Find Calm before Choosing Action

David knew about this phenomenon long before the advent of flight. He knew he must move into a realm of calm before he chose a course of action, so he strengthened himself in the Lord. David's previous experiences had prepared him for this. Surely he would never forget the day Samuel came to Jesse's house to choose a king (1 Samuel 16). All the boys marched out before the prophet. Eliab was very impressive, as were some of the others, but none were chosen. Even Samuel was dismayed when God didn't select any of them. Samuel even had to ask Jesse if he had any more sons. That was when they remembered David who was out keeping the sheep. He was too young, too short, too inexperienced, too unqualified. But, as he stood before the prophet, God indicated that this was his choice for the next king of Israel. Samuel poured the anointing oil on his head and the job was done.

David went back to his job of shepherding sheep, but he would not forget the lesson of that day: " . . . man looks on the outward appearance, but the LORD looks on the heart" (1 Samuel 16:7). The people had chosen Saul because he looked impressive, with all the personality, charisma, looks and charm expected of a king. But he had proven to be a man who judged only by what his physical eyes could see. One time Saul watched his enemies gather in increasing numbers while his own forces diminished, he wrongly concluded that it was acceptable for him to act as priest to make sacrifice. Another time when Saul saw the good sheep and goats of the Amalekites, he likewise concluded they would be good to keep, even though he had been commanded to kill them all. Saul could not see beyond the observational, and he thought with a mind committed to the appearance of success. Saul even asked Samuel to keep from the people the news of his awful disobedience. Now, through Samuel, God was picking the least apparent candidate to be his king. David noticed and learned. Reality is not always apparent!

The first priority in facing any circumstance is to see the reality behind the appearance. For instance, Jesus said to Nicodemus, ". . . unless one is born again he cannot see the kingdom of God" (John 3:3). "Seeing" was the point. And Paul explained how he was able to rejoice in the midst of the sufferings he faced.

> *Therefore, having this ministry by the mercy of God, we do not lose heart . . . For this light momentary affliction is preparing for us an eternal weight of glory beyond all comparison, as we look not to the things that are seen but to the things that are unseen. For the things that are seen are transient, but the things that are unseen are eternal.*
>
> 2 Corinthians 4:1, 17-18

God prepares us as he did David, orchestrating circumstances that obscure the obvious so we will seek reality behind the apparent.

The Privilege of Seeing the Unseen

Since we are citizens of the kingdom of God, we are not limited to observing the apparent. We have grace to see the unseen. This sight was the common equipment given to mankind in the Garden. Adam and Eve were aware of both worlds and of the interconnection between the seen and the unseen. After their fall into sin, mankind was cut off from God's revelation and began to operate almost exclusively on the observable. On occasion mankind would (illegally) venture into the mystic realm of the spirit to gain information from the deceiver. Fortune telling, tea-leaves, and magic became popular means of access for fallen men and women who needed more than the apparent, but could no longer obtain it from God. When we are brought to the end of ourselves and don't know what to do, we must see beyond the natural. This is one of the benefits God gives his people.

In the Old Testament, God gave his people a way to gain insight beyond the observable. They had priests who maintained the ephod, the Urim and Thummim. They had prophets who heard words and delivered them to the people. Wise men had dreams, and God gave them interpretation. All of these partial methods pointed to the full restoration that would come in the living Word of God. Jesus came into the world demonstrating how man could see what God revealed and act on a more complete knowledge than that of fallen man. Jesus lived focused on the reality behind the apparent. His disciples didn't understand, and the crowds thought he was mad. He never gave in to secondary causes and was not distracted by people who defined reality incorrectly nor by the forces of Satan who defined reality deceptively. He always responded first to God the Father, then he handled the devil or the people based on the information he received from the Father.

Wisdom is the term the Bible uses to describe God's perspective. Solomon was known as the wisest man of his day, and his wisdom came from seeing eyes and hearing ears. He was attuned to the revelation only God grants. Of course, the wisdom of Solomon is a partial picture of the full wisdom revealed in the greater Solomon, Christ. "And because of him you are in Christ Jesus, who became to us wisdom from God . . ." (1 Corinthians 1:30).

We are blessed to be in Christ, through whom the Father gives us the benefits only Christ deserves. He has thus granted us the privilege of seeing with eyes of faith. He has said that wisdom is ours for the asking. James, says in regard to responding to trials, "If any of you lacks wisdom, let him ask God, who gives generously to all without reproach, and it will be given him" (James 1:5). There is no reason for us to be limited to the apparent, unless we fail to take advantage of the grace offered.

We live in a world enamored with the apparent. We "spin" all facts for their best impact on perceptions. We choose our heroes based on looks and personality. Our church leaders are those who have the most people in their group. We measure a person's greatness on the basis of what he or she has built, what they have accumulated, or what positions they have held.

Recently a friend told me of two funerals he attended in the same week. One of the deceased was a man known internationally for the things he built. He developed many projects and his name and reputation were connected with tall buildings and sprawling centers. He sat on many influential boards and accumulated great wealth. Many people at his memorial service spoke of his achievements. The other deceased was a man who lived quietly and simply but was committed to making true disciples of Jesus. He spent lots of time with men and their wives helping them to walk with Christ. At his memorial service, the minister asked, "How many of you are in the kingdom of God today and owe your growth to this man?" Almost the whole congregation stood and applauded. Perhaps each man carried out his assignment, but we seem to hold the first one up as the model and ignore the second. We habitually judge by the apparent.

Without divine revelation we draw incorrect conclusions regarding what is important. We can't know God without his gracious revelation. No man could ever dream up the complex simplicity of grace. God is a mere projection of man's mind until God opens that mind to reveal his truth.

We cannot even know ourselves without this revelation. We see ourselves incompletely. We identify ourselves according to ethnicity, geography, philosophy, or education. Yet God identifies us only according to faith in Jesus his Son. Unless he shows us, we cannot even know what God is doing in our lives at the moment. Fortunately, he does show us because he does not hesitate to reveal necessary insight to anyone who is ready to obey. Now, to the idly curious he gives clues without explanation. And to the stubborn he gives information that leads to death. But to those who hunger for him, he gives sight beyond just the apparent.

Deliberate Calm Provides a New Perspective

What did David see when he took time to "strengthen himself in the Lord?" Perhaps he saw that Ziklag was his city, but he knew it was not the final one. Maybe he saw that God was allowing this city to be destroyed because Zion was in his future. Maybe he knew that he was not destined to lead a Philistine city; he was chosen to be king of the city of God. That city would be a type of the final city—the New Jerusalem that includes people from all over the world. Before he possessed the city of his destiny, Ziklag would have to burn.

(Some today who are still trying to rebuild the temple in Jerusalem destroyed in 70 AD. seem to miss the point that God has improved his temple. He has made us his living temple and the whole earth the temple mount.)

When God has revealed his perspective, we can enter into this deliberate calm. He is fully in charge and we are fully blessed, even if it doesn't appear that way. Not content just to write a book and leave us with printed instructions, our loving Father desires a living relationship in which he enjoys showing his sons and daughters what is theirs by virtue of their inheritance. Before we run off trying to fix our problem, killing Amalekites, blaming God and venting anger, let's move into the deliberate calm of God's presence.

3. More Grace at Ziklag

Many people I know are trying to recover from being blindsided by the economic downturn of the past few years. We can't help but ask questions: What did I do wrong? Is God not involved in the "secular" forces in the world? Why did he allow this to happen to innocent people who had nothing to do with Wall Street? Why didn't we see the warning signs and at least pull our money out before the crash?

And, of course, there are devastations beyond the economy. Divorce tears the hearts out of many people, including innocent children. Drug abuse paralyzes and undermines some of the most gifted people in our communities. Our daily lives are riddled with heartache, pain, disappointment and fear, often faced in dreadful isolation. Much of the world is waging wars or enduring governments run by madmen, while famine and disease kill off even more than the wars.

It is easy to retreat from life when we've been waylaid by the unexpected, whether it is on a global, national, or personal scale. Unanticipated trouble addles us with fear. Unchecked, it becomes paralyzing depression.

David and Ziklag Again

I suspect David felt much the same and asked many of the same questions when he returned to his city of Ziklag to find it devastated and ransacked. He and his men had been on their way to fight, yet again, alongside the Philistines, but this time against Israel and King Saul. Some of the Philistine commanders had their doubts about David's loyalties—at least in fighting against his countrymen, so his cohort was sent home. During the three days they were away, the Amalekites had attacked and burned Ziklag and carried away all the warriors' families as prisoners.

Imagine what a harsh blow this was to David. He was trying to survive until God kept his promise to make him Israel's king. He had been faithful to the Philistine king, fighting his enemies with courage and loyalty. He had done the best he could as he spent nearly fourteen years waiting for his destiny. And now, for no apparent reason, he had to face the loss of all his property and all his family, not to mention the additional losses of his men. How should he respond to the devastation of Ziklag?

The Privilege of Access

As we look over David's life we discover some lessons he had learned that allowed him to survive Ziklag. First of all, as we noted in the previous chapter, he reveled in the privilege of access. He went straight to God, knowing the door was open and he was welcome. He had spent days and nights tending his father's sheep. Those experiences taught him that God was his shepherd and intensely involved with his sheep.

For us the message is monumental. Jesus made it clear that because of him we have the same access to the Father he had (John 14:15-25). There is never a right time to run away from God, but especially not in difficult times. It is foolish and destructive. He knows everything about our circumstances and our struggle against them, but when we cut him out of our consciousness we are left with an unmanageable world. We often protest, "I can't pray. I don't even know what to say." But that is not a problem since his Spirit will even pray for us when we don't know what to pray (Romans 8:26-28). "But he seems far away and uninterested," we might protest. Yet by faith we know he is more interested in encountering us than we are in encountering him. After all, he created us for constant encounters. And when we sinned he made reconciliation available, at the expense of his own Son. He pursued us for relationship by sending his Spirit to convict and convert us. So now are we to conclude that he has gone on vacation leaving no forwarding address? He alone has what we need, and until we make that first step toward him, we are wasting time.

Recalling God's Faithfulness

Another thing we know about David is he often revisited the faithfulness of God. Before his showdown with Goliath, when asked why he thought he could defeat such a giant, he reminded the army of Israel that God had been with him when he fought a lion and a bear that had attacked his father's sheep. He had the confidence of a man who had seen God work in his realm of responsibility before. We have his psalms as record of his confidence in God's commitment to him. One of the most familiar is a good example:

GOD, my shepherd!
I don't need a thing.
You have bedded me down in lush meadows,
you find me quiet pools to drink from.
True to your word,
you let me catch my breath
and send me in the right direction.

Even when the way goes through
Death Valley,
I'm not afraid
when you walk at my side.
Your trusty shepherd's crook
makes me feel secure.

You serve me a six-course dinner
right in front of my enemies.
You revive my drooping head;
my cup brims with blessing.

Your beauty and love chase after me
every day of my life.
I'm back home in the house of GOD
for the rest of my life.

Psalms 23 (The Message)

We tend to focus on our own faithfulness (or faithless-ness) rather than God's faithfulness. If things go badly, we ramp up our level of commitment, promising God we will do better.

Bob Simpson lived in the community in which I grew up. Bob succumbed to the temptation to generate quick cash by making illegal moonshine. However, it wasn't long before the "Revenuers" started investigating, looking for stills like Bob's. Several men in the area were convicted and sentenced to prison. One day, as we all stood around the gas pumps at the country store—Bob included—the topic turned to the ongoing investigation. Even as a small boy, I still remember watching and listening to Bob's promises. He was nervous and pale, swearing before witnesses that if God would get him out of this mess, he would never do such a thing again. He promised to be in the fields every day doing his work and in church on Sundays. It made an impression on me, and several times in my life I have tried Bob's strategy for dealing with my sins. I would promise God never to do it again if only he would forgive me and not let me get caught. Sometimes I wasn't caught and other times I was. But I know now that this is no way to strengthen yourself in the Lord.

It's God's promises that matter, not our level of commitment. He has demonstrated his desire and intention to bless us. He first promised Abraham that he would bless him and his seed so that blessings would come to all. Those blessings were culminated in Jesus, who is the consummate Seed of Abraham. Those of us who are "in Christ" are heirs of the blessing bestowed on him. God has ordered all of history to testify of his faithfulness in blessing his people.

God demonstrates his faithfulness by keeping his promises and fulfilling his oaths. The author of Hebrews is inspired to say that God, wanting to show his strong commitment to blessing us, swore (or made an oath) by himself.

> *For when God made a promise to Abraham, since he had no one greater by whom to swear, he swore by himself saying, "Surely I will bless you and multiply you."*

> Hebrews 6:13-14

God is faithful to himself. For him to cease being favorable toward his people, he would have to break his promise to himself. God holds himself accountable for his promise to bless. What a mind-blowing reality!

Blessed Beyond Any Doubt

Alan Wright points out that when we doubt our blessed-ness in God, we do stupid things. Adam and Eve were convinced by the tempter that they were not fully blessed, so they sinned by attempting to get more blessings. Cain concluded that he was not blessed like his brother, and that eventually led him to murder his brother. David's adultery and murder began when he saw Bathsheba and concluded that he was not fully blessed unless he had her.

On the other hand, when we are confident of our stand-ing with God and sure of our blessing, we attempt great things in faith. This was David's motivation for taking on Goliath. The ultimate example, of course, is Jesus' victory over death in his crucifixion and resurrection. In John 13, we learn that Jesus takes the towel and washes his disciple's feet, "knowing that the Father had given all things into his hands, and that he had come from God and was going back to God" (John 13:3). In the same way we express true humility because of our confidence in what Jesus has done and promised. Only when we have confidence based on his faithfulness are we ready to move to the next phase and seek guidance in decision-making.

After David had strengthened himself in the Lord he went to the priest and sought God's direction in response to his situation. God assured him through the priest's ephod that he should pursue the enemy and rescue his people. We don't need the priest's ephod today, but we should consult

God through his appointed means: the senses, the saints, and the Scriptures as illuminated by the Spirit.

In this story David draws a sketch that previews the coming portrait of Jesus. While awaiting the day of his coronation, he was stripped of everything by the enemy. Being strengthened in the Spirit, he went to the realm of the enemy and rescued his people. He was crowned king over God's people and rules over God's sphere. We have this confidence: The greater "David" lives in us to expand his kingdom to the boundaries purchased by his sacrifice. We can strengthen ourselves with even greater confidence than Israel's David.

4. Kingdom Economics

Most things in life are beyond our control. Markets go up, and then down; neighbors are nice, then contrary; the weather is sunny, then stormy; life is easy, then it turns crazy. When life is so unstable, we look for the unshakable. The New Testament speaks to this phenomenon:

At that time his voice shook the earth, but now he has promised, "Yet once more I will shake not only the earth but also the heavens." This phrase, "Yet once more," indicates the removal of things that are shaken—that is, things that have been made—in order that the things that cannot be shaken may remain. Therefore let us be grateful for receiving a kingdom that cannot be shaken, and thus let us offer to God acceptable worship, with reverence and awe, for our God is a consuming fire.

Hebrews 12:26-29

God originally gave the basis of his kingdom order to Israel, but through the years Israel added to it and distorted it. When the epistle to the Hebrews was written, all of the expectations, assumptions, traditions and institutions that had grown up around those distortions were about to be shaken and reordered. Jesus had come as the fulfillment of Israel's hopes, but Israel had rejected him. He was not what they had pictured, and his kingdom was not what they expected. Within a generation God shook down the edifice that had been built around the previously simple kingdom, and began again with a few motley disciples of Jesus as the pillars of a new order. God is always willing to expose the unnecessary so that we can embrace the essential. Whatever else is going on with the turmoil in the world's economy or society, we can be sure God is shaking his people so they can discover what's unshakable.

The King Alone Determines the Outcomes

The Lord has established his throne in the heavens, and his kingdom rules over all.

Psalms 103:19

God's kingdom allows for no contingencies. We don't have to worry about secondary causes. We work with them, but they do not determine ultimate outcomes. Governments, markets, people and places are part of the picture, but in the ultimate outcome, these things are simply chess pieces that will yield to the purpose of the Master.

Some people are terribly worried about the devil; they are sure he is stirring up things and bears the responsiblity for their troubles. Others are angry with the government for disrupting their comfort zone. Though these players are involved—and we must be responsible in our dealings with them—they cannot override the final outcome of God's promise and purpose.

Kingdom of Covenant

Our God has always worked with a covenant people. All the previous covenants in the Old Testament looked forward to a final new covenant that would fulfill them. Covenants, by design, have partners with responsibilities to each other. The problem with the earlier covenants was the people's inability to fulfill their responsibilities. Yet in the new covenant, Jesus took on the role of the people and fully lived up to all that was required. So those who trust him as their representative gain the benefits of a covenant fully kept. Nothing can diminish the inheritance of believers because their benefits depend solely on the qualifications of Jesus, their representative. There are no alternative plans; those who trust Jesus receive the covenant promises.

For this is the covenant that I will make with the house of Israel after those days, declares the Lord: I will put my laws into their minds, and I will be their God, and they shall be my people. And they shall not teach, each one his neighbor and each one his brother, saying, "Know the Lord," for they shall all know me, from the least of them to the greatest. For

I will be merciful toward their iniquities, and I will remember their sins no more.

Hebrews 12:10-12

God's original covenant with Abraham was all about bringing a blessing on the earth instead of a curse. He told Abraham that he would be the father of a nation that would produce a Seed who would redeem the earth from the curse brought upon it through Adam's sin. It took two thousand years, but the Seed (Jesus) finally came and made the transfer of blessings possible. He took upon himself the sentence of guilt. He then commissioned his disciples to go to the whole world with the message of the good news: A new creation has begun. There is hope. Anyone can be forgiven and become the child of God the Father. He is willing to take us on as his covenant partner with all the requirements already met for us. He will be our God and we will belong to his people. He is taking responsibility for us.

Nothing can prevent God from being as committed to us as he is to his only begotten Son. Regardless of the currency, the culture or the climate, we are in covenant with God Almighty, who rules over all.

Fatherly Kingdom

Therefore do not be anxious, saying, 'What shall we eat?' or 'What shall we drink?' or 'What shall we wear?' For the Gentiles seek after all these things, and your heavenly Father knows that you need them

*all. But seek first the kingdom of God and his right-
eousness, and all these things will be added to you.*

Matthew 6:32-33

It can never be said of God that he doesn't take care of his children. No demon in hell could make that rumor stick. History proves that when God takes on a people as his sons they are supported abundantly. No one in the neighborhood of the universe will be able to accuse God the Father with neglect of his family. His kids are furnished with everything they need to accomplish their assignments. They might not impress the fashion mavens, but they will be supplied even in famine (Psalms 37:18-19). Someone may object that his kids don't often deserve it, but the terms of the covenant still stand. Their treatment is based on the merits of Jesus alone. Case settled. Others might object that they have seen good Christians suffer hunger, neglect, persecution or homelessness. Remember that when the crowd saw Jesus on the cross they concluded that God the Father was not caring for him. They misinterpreted the situation. Jesus committed himself into the hands of the Father in total trust. God's greater purpose can't be judged by physical evidence alone.

In God's Kingdom, his giving nature is featured and his people are taught that real wealth is discovered in generosity. Hard times reveal the difference between those who are true givers and those who merely give out of surplus.

[G]ive and it will be given to you. Good measure, pressed down, shaken together, running over, will be put into your lap.

Luke 6:38

God sees to it that when his children give, he gives more. This precept will not be violated because God is the ultimate source, and his inventory is eternally full. Our tendency in shaky circumstances is to hold back and hoard out of fear. Those who try to hold on to what they have, never have enough to be secure. But those who are aware of their partnership with God the Father are not afraid of lack. They only want to fulfill his assignment, and they consciously work with a supply mentality. They never have so little that they can't invest.

God is the ultimate giver, and he enables us to imitate him. He spotlights the givers and releases more to their care. Those who try to use this insight to manipulate the kingdom for their own greed expose themselves as getters and eventually become disgruntled with the promise. God gives to *givers*, not just to someone who is working a deal. Verse 35 should be read in conjunction with 38, "But love your enemies and do good, and lend expecting nothing in return and your reward will be great and you will be sons of the most high."

The reward is inevitable, but the motive for giving is not getting something in return. The motive for giving is love. It is to display the character of God's sons. Sons care more about honoring their father than making a deal!

The Influence of the Faithful

One who is faithful in a very little is also faithful in much, and one who is dishonest in a very little is also dishonest in much. If then you have not been faithful in the unrighteous wealth, who will entrust to you the true riches?

Luke 16:10-11

Since God wants the whole creation to experience the blessings of his kingdom, he is looking for those who want to expand. He loves to include us in expansion, but the way we get to participate is by being faithful in what he's already given to us. If we are not using it to bless the earth and glorify him, why should he give us more? On the other hand, if we are faithful with what we have, nothing can stop God from expanding our influence as he deems best. Those who want more stuff to bolster their poor sense of significance are trying to expand for the wrong reasons. God may allow them to acquire more than some would think is just, but take care because sometimes God gives us what we want as judgment. Stuff doesn't satisfy for long. It will eventually make our stomachs turn.

Everyone has been given something to steward. No one has been left out. Time spent standing around comparing what is in my hand to what is in your hand and then feeling inferior because I want yours and devalue mine is wasted and wicked time. The key to my growth is using what I already have. I have the seeds of wealth and power in my hands right now, but I must submit to the King of the kingdom to know how to manage it for his purposes.

Servants Are the Greatest

And Jesus called them to him and said to them, "You know that those who are considered rulers of the Gentiles Lord it over them, and their great ones exercise authority over them. But it shall not be so among you. But whoever would be great among you must be our servant, and whoever would be first among you must be servant of all."

Mark 10:42-44

Each of us is born with a desire to be significant—a desire only truly satisfied when we find a servant's heart. Doing some good things periodically may give a temporary thrill, but having our hearts radically changed so that we actually live to serve is a transformation that brings true satisfaction. Those who have been born of the Spirit of God have that heart. Many have not fully uncovered it because they have bought into the culture's way of determining who is great. But when they renew their thoughts and release their inner heart, they begin to live. Nothing can stop God from elevating to true greatness those who serve. It is not dependent on sharp bosses or good circumstances. It is an unshakable truth. God alone oversees promotion—even in hard times.

The shaking we experience is our friend. It exposes the things that should never be trusted and reveals what must be trusted. It is our privilege and responsibility to embrace the unshakable values and build our lives on them. To fail to do so is foolish and deadly. While we work, play, earn, invest, save, vote, and spend, let's do so with the intent to honor the king that rules over all.

5. Why Does Victory Feel Like Defeat?

Jesse came to see me—discouraged and wanting to talk. He had once been excited about knowing Christ and being filled with the Holy Spirit. He was thrilled when he saw early prayers answered, people healed and delivered from bondage. But now he was confused by the constant trouble in his path. Issues with family, finances, and personal holiness kept cropping up, so he felt defeated because he couldn't live in "victory."

Sarah called to talk. She had been attracted to the ministry of a very charismatic leader with great communication skills. He always had some new exotic insight or novel interpretation of Scripture. His followers were sure they knew secrets about the Bible that ordinary people didn't. His message had promised that if they would buy into it, they would have the best life, free from the entanglements of Satan's schemes. She had been assured that by following certain principles her life would be blessed. After being involved for seven years, she finally admitted that it wasn't working. No matter how hard she tried to believe and behave better, she was losing the battle.

I saw Jim at church. He had lost his job due to cutbacks at his company. It had shaken him, and he had realized that God was confronting him with his selfish ambition and workaholic nature. He had trouble knowing how to wait and rest in the Lord. Some Christian friends had told him to just pray and wait, while others told him he should look for a job. He wasn't sure where to draw the line between laziness and resting.

My friends are probably a lot like some of yours in their confusion and discouragement. We know Jesus has won the final victory but is there any place in Scripture that tells us how to deal with what feels like defeat in life's daily struggles? In 2 Corinthians 10-12, Paul addressed what was for him an awkward situation. He had to defend his apostleship to the believers in Corinth because some "false apostles" had come there seeking to pull them away from the gospel Paul had proclaimed. These pretenders were denouncing Paul as their inferior, and their evidence was that he was constantly in problematic circumstances. He had spent time in jail, had been rejected by civic and religious leaders in several provinces, and had a chronic physical ailment that threatened his effectiveness at times. He had also been stoned, shipwrecked and left without food or water, and he had to work for his own sustenance. These "superior" ministers concluded that Paul would not be experiencing such "defeats" if he had the "victory of faith."

In defending his ministry, Paul articulates a perspective imperceptible to people who measure success by natural standards. Our sinful hearts and darkened minds measure strength in terms of personal achievement and popular acclaim, but Paul had learned a better way:

If I must boast, I will boast of the things that show my weakness.

2 Corinthians 11:30

False Prophets Expose Immaturity by Appealing to Lower Motivation

Several recent reports of scientific studies decry the obesity found among many children in the U.S. Part of the problem is that American children love fast food. Expert marketers have trained us to like grease and fat so we will purchase their products. There was a time when advertising was about offering products that met consumer needs, but not any more. Now marketers use their expertise to elicit a need for products by training the public to want and like what they sell. You won't see a lot of commercials for eggs, fruit, and protein, but watch Saturday morning cartoons, and you just have to have an Egg McMuffin or a McGriddle with syrup.

Sadly, the gospel has been marketed by the same methods. Whole churches and ministries have trained people to prefer fast-food-style spirituality. As a result we are drawn to celebrity leaders, thornless roses, natural success, majority opinion and spiritual elitism. We value impressive résumés over proven character, and we listen to television interviewers and preachers, athletes, and movie stars as if their perspectives matter more than those of an elderly grandfather who has lived a long, hard life and lived it well. Those with celebrity status are granted great authority to influence our thinking and our decisions. So at church we buy the fast food of shallow sermons, sensational stories and sound-bite theology. These things suit our acquired tastes. They make us feel good in the moment or motivate us for the half-hour after church but leave us with a false idea of real purpose and thinking we can attain a pain-free and happy existence.

Something is clearly wrong. We try to satisfy an internal hunger that can only be met by the message of the genuine gospel. Obesity and starvation slowly encroach on our malnourished souls while we feed on a message created by a cross-less culture. But it doesn't satisfy. We seem to think that if we eat more of what is offered we will finally get well, but we just get sicker. Grease and fat do not nourish us no matter how much we consume. We long for extraordinary spiritual experiences, but often for the wrong reasons.

The false prophets of Corinth were using their unusual "revelations" as leverage to gain authority over the believers. Paul too had an extraordinary experience and saw things he could not tell. (What would be the fun in that?) Whatever he saw and heard turned him into a servant who refused to use his credentials to impress. He did not want others to think more highly than his own person warranted. In contrast, the trend among our church leaders is to impress so that people will follow and help build their ministries. Résumés are altered and reputations are exaggerated in order to gain leverage

Paul did not want that kind of leverage. He was obsessed with the gospel of Jesus. He confronted Peter and contradicted any other preacher who diminished the gospel in order to appease someone. Whatever Paul saw in his visionary experience made him radically passionate about the gospel of Jesus Christ. He was absolutely convinced that the gospel must be proclaimed and protected if God's purpose was to be accomplished through the church. He refused to mix Greek oratorical rhetoric with the gospel, and he was willing to be called a poor speaker as a result. He would not allow the circumcision party to add to the simple gospel, and it cost him dearly as he was threatened, accused, beaten, jailed, and stoned for it.

And remember, the extraordinary revelations were related to Paul's "thorn in the flesh." God gave him the thorn, using Satan's messenger, to prevent conceit. I sometimes wonder if those who are so anxious to visit the third heaven have thought about the ramifications. It could be that the very reasons we think it is great are the very reasons we couldn't handle it. From what we know of Paul's life, what he saw messed him up for any celebrity-style Christianity.

Who Creates False Prophets?

We wouldn't have false prophets if there were no market for them. People trained to consume religious fast-food demand a certain kind of leader. He or she must produce what tastes good to our malnourished souls. They must perform as saviors, healers, fathers, fix-it men, and celebrities. They aren't allowed to look common or act naturally. They must not make mistakes, and they must compete with entertainers and professional speakers for our attention. Their message must always be positive and never mention the consequences of negative choices or the harsh realities of life.

If they are musicians, they must play and sing the fast-food music we like to hear. The lyrics don't have to carry any theological meaning as long as they sound good and have some kind of rhyme. As long as the band on the stage is loud and contemporary, we in the congregation are content to vicariously worship through them. So the musicians as well as the preachers have become false prophets in the sense that they are meeting market demands but ignoring the heart of the gospel.

Like the false apostles of Paul's day, today's consumers demand that leaders be triumphal. They might have to deny limitations or hide weaknesses, and must always smile and say the right things. So a leader who wants to succeed is strongly tempted to become the figure his public demands.

Who loses out in this arrangement? First, the consumer loses spiritual nutrition as he or she continues to consume more and more religious stuff hoping for relief. Eventually, there are not enough Bible studies, television programs, church activities, or praise songs to do the job. Actually, there is just not enough time to take it all in. Then the leaders themselves lose. If they have truly been called to proclaim the gospel, they begin to feel like prostitutes. Without the satisfaction of exalting Christ, they settle for building (or trying to build) larger personal kingdoms. After years of less than they expected, they cry, "Burnout!" Fading into the sunset of their ministry, they wonder if it was all worth it.

Worst of all, the Lord himself is diminished because Jesus gave himself for the gospel. It alone is the power of God unto salvation, and when it is not proclaimed and practiced, the glory of the cross is dishonored. When the gospel is not held high, the glory of Christ is not seen. When Christ is not exalted, the purpose of God is not fulfilled. When the purpose of God is not fulfilled, the nations suffer. There is no winner except hell when we adopt the value system of false apostles or false prophets. But remember, without a market there would be no proliferation of consumer-oriented preachers.

God's Design: Exalt Jesus through Weaknesses

Even Paul was susceptible to conceit when given special privilege (thus the need for the thorn in his flesh). No one is immune to pride. Remember Israel, the least of all nations? God granted them special privilege and they interpreted it as leverage. Paul was given such high-level revelations he could not reveal them. Imagine what kind of intrigue he could have created in mass meetings if he had even hinted that he was somehow special because of how God had spoken to him. But the gospel was too important for that. God gave him something to counteract that temptation.

What was it that Paul called "a thorn in the flesh?" We don't know for sure, but it was something he would rather have done without. It was an affliction he prayed to be delivered from. It was not a habitual sin, but it was something that exposed his desperate need for God's grace. It made people need to look beyond his personal appearance or performance to see who he really was. If you looked only at the surface, you would have missed the real Paul. It was somehow potentially offensive to some in the church. Yet those who could see beyond the surface knew they were dealing with a spiritual heavyweight, a man who didn't need a résumé to establish his authority. He walked with the authority that comes from grace in time of need. His weakness had made room for a grace more powerful than man's titles could convey.

We prefer a deliverance that prevents any affliction requiring faith. We prefer for grace to mean a lack of problems and suffering. But whatever deliverance is, it doesn't render us free enough to neglect our daily dependence on Jesus. Grace gives us the ability to walk through afflictions.

He will never fix us so well that we don't need his fellowship. We are delivered into dependence on him, and whatever moves us in that direction is a great gift from God, even when delivered by Satan's messenger.

Once the thorn is recognized as a gift, we can be confident in grace rather than defeated by affliction. With this perspective, we can wait without passivity and work without idolatry. Our privilege is to respond to him daily and to enjoy our journey with him. Numbers and activity are not the measure of our success. So we can be as content to work with one person in private as with thousands in public, knowing we are working where he is working. Resting in his sovereignty allows us to act with purpose and hope and still avoid the passivity of fatalism. We can also enjoy watching the fruit of labor when he works through us. It is not our responsibility to make things happen. It is our privilege to be apart of what God is making happen. Our excitement grows as we observe the gospel actually transforming people and their cultures, so we want to be even more involved.

When we refuse to acknowledge our thorns, or constantly complain about them, we reveal that our purpose is less than exalting Christ. We are demanding a thorn-free existence. When we believe, preach, and embrace the true gospel, which is a victorious gospel, we are content for it to be expressed through our weaknesses. Like our Lord who on Friday appeared weak on the cross, we may appear to be weak to those who can't see. But we know about the coming

Sunday! What feels like defeat might just be our greatest victory.

Conclusion

I have spent some time around those who are enamored with hard times. As the ole country song goes, "If it weren't for bad luck, I'd have no luck at all." Well, for some if they had no hard times, they would have no story to tell. I sometimes wonder if they feature this because it somehow assuages their guilt over sin. That is not what this book is about; we don't glory in hard times in order to tell a better story than the next guy (the way old people compare their surgeries). We glory in the grace of God that excels in the midst of what we call hard times.

We have not sought to find a checklist of survival techniques in the midst of hard times. Those lists may help, but usually they prolong the process of coming to the end of our own resources and discovering those given to us by God.

We are rejoicing in the grace of our Lord Jesus who rules to bring about the sure and good purpose of God the Father. He is working in and through all circumstances to reveal the fullest measure of grace that we can handle. Our hope is in his faithfulness as our eternal high priest and our supreme reigning King. He has proven that Hell cannot concoct a scheme that deters his purpose or depletes his grace. We are the beneficiaries of his life that fulfills all covenant requirements, his death that settles all penalties, his resurrection defeats death and assures us of immortality, and his ascension that guarantees his beneficial sovereignty toward us. Now having received the same spirit that raised him from the dead, we are empowered to live in the midst of this world with unquenchable faith and unending love.

About the Author

Dudley Hall is a recognized teacher who has been blessed with extraordinary gifts for equipping the body of Christ. He holds a Masters of Divinity from Southwestern Baptist Theological Seminary and a Bachelors degree from Samford University. Dudley's formal ministry began in college leading youth evangelism crusades. Sensing a need for discipleship training beyond the initial "sinner's prayer" experience, he developed a follow-up program to citywide evangelistic crusades that touched thousands. He has helped plant churches throughout the United States and Africa and was a founder of the Emmaus Road Ministry School.

Dudley is passionate about the centrality of Jesus Christ and the proclamation and practice of the New Testament Gospel. He mentors young men, business leaders, pastors and ministry leaders, connecting the generations in a single-minded pursuit of knowing the Father as only a son can. Dudley is gifted in empowering men to embrace their masculine spirituality and leadership roles. His teaching and discipleship materials are used around the world.

Dudley has authored several books including *Grace Works*, *Incense & Thunder*, *Glad to be Left Behind*, *Orphans No More*, and *Men In Their Own Skin*. He is a sought-after speaker, an engaging preacher, an effective consultant, and a trusted spiritual father. Dudley is the founder and President of Successful Christian Living

Ministries (SCLM) now known as Kerygma Ventures, through which he leads a network of churches, pastors and ministry leaders called Kerygma Network as well as producing discipleship materials and training programs. Dudley is most at home on the beautiful 350-acre Tesoro Escondido Ranch discipling and training leaders in all spheres of life. Dudley and his wife, Betsy, live in Grapevine, Texas. They have two grown children and five grandkids.

www.kerygmaventures.com

The Gospel.
There are two words used to describe the greatest message ever delivered. The most common word is *euangelion* translated into English as *evangel*. It refers to good news. Of course the good news of the New Testament is that God has fulfilled his promise and the kingdom has come. It has amazing ramifications for all who hear and believe. The second word is *kerygma*. It carries the sense of a herald announcing an event—and by announcing it, bringing it into being. Though the two words are closely linked, *kerygma* became the designation for the essential, irreducible elements of the apostolic message of the New Testament church. When Jesus arrived, it became clear that there was something new and different about the message he preached. Not only did he announce that the greatest day in history—the day all Israel had hoped for—had come, he inaugurated it. He didn't just give facts and tell stories. He was the message. In his address in the synagogue in Nazareth, he announced that he was the fulfillment of what Isaiah had prophesied. He was not making a prediction. He was instituting the ultimate Year of Jubilee. His proclamation was more than a word spoken. It was God's word in action.

The apostles of the New Testament saw their proclamation as being the instruments through which Christ preached the kingdom. They were not just telling about Jesus, his teachings, and his miracles. He was present in their preaching, and thus those who heard them would either embrace him or reject him. To some it would be scandalous. To others it would be foolish. But to those who could hear, it was supernatural power and divine wisdom (1 Corinthians 1:21-25). Paul refused to let traditional oratory or human persuasion get in the way of the message. He wanted the fruit of the proclamation to be personal faith rather than understanding or applause.

I. Jesus Christ fulfilled Old Testament promise and prophecy.
The content of the kerygma is the message that when proclaimed, makes something happen. It begins with the announcement that the time has been fulfilled and the kingdom has arrived. A new day has dawned. The era of hope and anticipation has been eclipsed with the fulfillment of the promises. The day the earth had been anticipating since the Garden of Eden arrived in Jesus. The future invaded the present and made it possible for believers to live in the present with the life of the future.

II. The incarnation, death and resurrection of Jesus Christ inaugurated a New Covenant through which forgiveness of sin is accessible and complete.
The *kerygma* includes the reality that sins are forgiven—forever. In the past sins were remitted based on the sacrificial system in place through Moses' covenant. They were "pushed forward" as it were. With the crucifixion and resurrection, sins were declared forgiven. People who are forgiven do not have to be sin-conscious anymore. All that sin had prevented in mankind's relation to God was restored. We can enter the most holy place. We can converse with holy God. The holy blood of Christ has washed our consciences. We can again partner with God in subduing the earth for his glory.

III. The Holy Spirit, as the sign and seal of adoption, empowers believers to live in joyful obedience.
The proclamation of Jesus' resurrection signifies not only that holy God has accepted the sacrifice Jesus offered, but also that the presence of the same Spirit that raised Jesus from the dead dwells within us. Jesus sent the Holy Spirit to provide the basis of hope for personal transformation and eternal immortality. His presence guarantees our adoption as sons of the Father and enables us to put to death the things of the flesh to live in the power of the Spirit.

IV. The invasion of the kingdom of God produces a new kind of people.
The people of God are not defined by geography, ethnicity, nationality, or gender. They are people marked by the Spirit of God. The law of God has been imprinted on their hearts, and their behavior is characterized by

a determination to love as Christ loved. They live in mutual submission recognizing they are members of Christ's visible body on earth now. They are commissioned to represent him as responsible managers and priests to the ends of the earth.

V. The presence of the king demands a response.

Jesus is the fulfillment of all previous types and shadows; he is the only mediator between God and man; therefore he is the judge of all things. All blessings in this era are related to and found in him. When he is present everything bows to his Lordship. For this reason, when the gospel is proclaimed a response is required. Repentance is required— not because of the badness of mankind—but because of the presence of the kingdom of God. He demands a choice. The process of seeing greater dimensions of the kingdom means that repentance continues at least through the entire life of every believer.

Kerygma speaks to the content of our message and the solemnity of our mission. We are under mandate to announce what God has done in Christ with all its ramifications. We are also under constraint to accurately proclaim and practice nothing beyond and nothing short of his gospel. If we just preach about him or his teachings, we fail. We must present him. In the power of the Spirit, we expect his word to accomplish what it always does when it goes forth. The miracles that accompany his word will affirm that he is still proclaiming the arrival of the kingdom of God.

Kerygma Ventures hosts a number of discipleship training programs at our Tesoro Escondido Ranch facility near Mineral Wells, Texas. For more information about any of these programs, please check the Kerygma Ventures website at www.kerygmaventures.com

Father & Son Weekend

The relationship between father and son is one of the most important aspects of godly manhood. This retreat is designed to bridge the gap that our culture often places between fathers and sons by providing unique situations in which fathers and sons learn to communicate honestly and effectively. Activities include: rappelling, adventure games, campfire story-telling, prayer & worship. The culmination of the retreat is a special "Rites of Passage" ceremony in which fathers call their sons into the community of manhood. (Generally held in early June.)

Father & Daughter Weekend

The "daddy-daughter bond" is something so special yet so hard to explain. As women, our perceptions of ourselves and our destinies are wrapped up in the way we imagine our fathers view us. At the Father and Daughter Weekend we hope to provide an opportunity to explore and strengthen the "daddy-daughter" relationship by addressing some key issues including what a beautiful woman is, lies the culture tells us, our need for fatherly affirmation, and finding our destiny by seeing the Father's heart. (Generally held in mid-February.)

Wildman Texas

Wildman Texas is a sportsmen-oriented retreat featuring fly-fishing and turkey-calling seminars, a shotgunning workshop, and an archery course. This is a great opportunity to bring along a friend and enjoy the fellowship and fun in a casual, low-key environment.

Beyond Happiness…

What if God's purpose in marriage goes beyond some limited concept of self-fulfillment or personal happiness? (It does!) This couples retreat focuses on marriage from a Gospel perspective. While good technique is better than bad technique, the point of this retreat is to get beyond methodologies and skill sets and delve into the heart of the matter as we explore the implications of the Gospel for a man and woman coming together to illustrate God's love for his people.

The Five Pillars Retreat

The first five books of the Old Testament served as a basis for the life of God's people under the Old Covenant. While the Pentateuch laid the foundation for the instructions Israel would need to live as God's people, we now live in the New Covenant era where all the promises and predictions of the Old Testament are fulfilled in Christ. In the New Covenant era, there are five dynamics – five pillars of truth which are foundational for embracing the great salvation we received as sons of God through Christ. They are living pillars, working together to equip us to live the eternal life Jesus modeled for us and gave to us. The Five Pillars Retreat is a weekend discipleship experience taught by Dudley Hall focusing on one of the five pillars, its relationship to the other four, and application to and in the life of the believer.

Leadership Expedition

WWW.LEADERSHIPEXPEDITION.ORG - The vision for Leadership Expedition is to discover a special group of young men and invest in them the resources they will need to make an impact for the Kingdom of God in their generation. The men we are looking for have heard the call of God on their lives. They have answered it and counted the costs, and they are committed to doing what it takes to fulfill their God-ordained destiny by leading their generation to a greater realization of the Kingdom of God. Leadership Expedition seeks to impart to them a vision for the future, to equip them with the necessary tools for leadership, and to connect them with others who share their passion. If you know of a young man who might be interested in this type of training, please recommend him to us. (Generally held the middle of July.)

THE FIVE PILLARS OF NEW TESTAMENT DISCIPLESHIP

The word "discipleship" has had many interpretations and methodologies over the years as people have sought to obey the Great Commission Jesus gave us: "...go into all the world and make disciples." But what does it really mean to make disciples? What exactly are we to preach and teach? What are we to do? What do disciples look like?

True discipleship can be encompassed in five integrated topics that dynamically work together, feed each other and keep us growing in the process of living out Christ-centered lives. We've called them the Five Pillars of New Testament Discipleship.

PILLAR 1: ENJOYING GOD
Many times we focus on "Knowing" God, but is it possible to study about God and not enjoy Him? Unfortunately, it is. Many of us have misconceptions about God and His will or intentions for our lives, so we attempt to know about Him without ever developing a real relationship with Him. As a result we never get to the place of truly enjoying Him. This study will deal with some of the perceptions and misconceptions we have about God. As we engage Him in truth we will discover it is His intention that we really and truly enjoy Him, which makes discipleship fun rather than a struggle.

PILLAR 2: DISCOVERING TRUTH
Instead of viewing the Bible as a manual to be followed or a book of principles to be deciphered and applied by each culture, we see that it's a beautiful story. A true story. A story of a Father and a Son. A story that gives meaning and purpose—as well as hope and possibility. A story that includes you and me. A story worth reading, enjoying and living. The Bible is a story that changes us and gives us power to change the world around us. In these sessions, we learn how to approach this story and discover the truth and joy in the Scriptures.

PILLAR 3: MANAGING LIFE
The very way we live is changed by the application of the gospel. In these sessions we will learn how to make daily decisions consistent with the truth we discover about God's will, our purposes and passions, and our assignment in the Kingdom of God. This understanding will clear out the self-help books on your shelves, because we don't really need any more *self*-help. We simply need to understand and embrace the life

God has given us to live, and it's not hard. We have everything we need, and as we replace our orphan mindset with the perspective of sons we can even enjoy the process.

PILLAR 4: ENGAGING THE CULTURE

Contrary to popular opinion, our assignment is not to live a comfortable, successful, pain-free life here on earth while we wait for heaven. We have been given the job of bringing heaven to earth. We have a responsibility to understand the surrounding culture—not only to make wise decisions for our own lives, but also to bring reform. We will either be shaped by our culture or we will shape it. In these sessions we focus on how to engage culture and bring God's redemptive purposes to earth as they are in heaven.

PILLAR 5: EMBRACING DESTINY

People throughout the ages have asked, "What is my meaning and purpose?" We all want to have a reason for being. And we do! We are created with purpose and meaning. As we enjoy God, see the great story of the scriptures, manage our lives and change the culture around us, we discover our part in that big story. These sessions discuss the clues which help guide us into our specific callings.